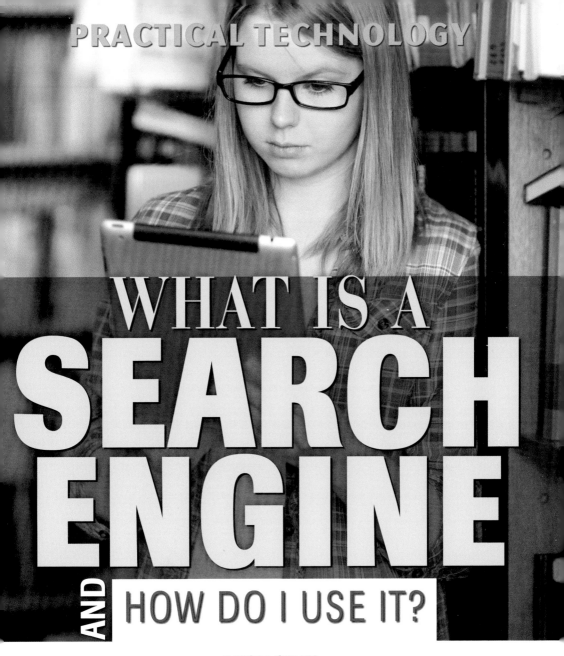

PRACTICAL TECHNOLOGY

WHAT IS A
SEARCH
ENGINE
AND HOW DO I USE IT?

LEON GRAY

Britannica
Educational Publishing

IN ASSOCIATION WITH

ROSEN
EDUCATIONAL SERVICES

Published in 2014 by Britannica Educational Publishing (a trademark of Encyclopædia Britannica, Inc.) in association with The Rosen Publishing Group, Inc.
29 East 21st Street, New York, NY 10010

Distributed exclusively by Rosen Publishing.
To see additional Britannica Educational Publishing titles, go to rosenpublishing.com

First Edition

Britannica Educational Publishing
J.E. Luebering: Director, Core Reference Group
Anthony L. Green: Editor, Compton's by Britannica

Rosen Publishing
Hope Lourie Killcoyne: Executive Editor
Nelson Sá: Art Director

Library of Congress Cataloging-in-Publication Data

Gray, Leon, 1974-
What is a search engine and how do I use it? / Leon Gray. — First edition.
    pages cm. — (Practical technology)
Audience: Grade 5 to 8.
Includes bibliographical references and index.
ISBN 978-1-62275-081-8 (library bound) — ISBN 978-1-62275-082-5 (paperback) — ISBN 978-1-62275-293-5 (6 pack)
1. Web search engines—Juvenile literature. I. Title.
TK5105.884.G73 2014
025.04252—dc23
                                        2013027179

Manufactured in the United States of America

Photo Credits
Cover: Shutterstock: Ermolaev Alexander. Inside: Dreamstime: Digitalgenetics 6, Fordprefect 36, Juliengrondin 42, Philcold 44, Wickedgood 27; Shutterstock: Ermolaev Alexander 1, Ariwasabi 4, David Arts 18, Olga Bogatyrenko 26, S Bukley 21, Drserg 7, Mike Flippo 34, Fotocromo 8, Darrin Henry 14–15, IM Photo 4bg, Iofoto 38, Herbert Kratky 22, Lenetstan 24, Lolloj 31, Monkey Business Images 35, Lukiyanova Natalia/Frenta 17, Carrie Nelson 29, Ioannis Pantzi 41, Rook76 33l, 33r, Annette Shaff 13, Sommthink 30, Ahmad Faizal Yahya 11, Zeber 25.

CONTENTS

A search engine is one of the most important tools you can use to find pages on the World Wide Web.

INTRODUCTION

A search engine is a tool that helps you find information on the Internet. The results of your search are displayed on a page called the Search Engine Results Page (SERP).

There is a vast amount of information on the Internet. Search engines make finding information quick and easy. They use computer programs to comb through the millions of pages on the web.

Search engines index the pages, which means they organize them into groups with similar content. One group could be all the pages about the president of the United States. Another group could be all the pages about a baseball team.

If you want to find out about movies at your local movie theater, for example, you can use a search engine, such as Google, to help you. When you type www.google.com into your Internet browser, the Google logo appears in the middle of the web page. If you type the name of your local movie theater in the search box, a list of pages about this theater will be displayed. Then, all you need to do is click on a page to see if it has the information you need.

CHAPTER 1

SEARCH ENGINE HISTORY

The World Wide Web is part of the Internet. Using a computer connected to the Internet and a web browser, you can access websites. Search engines help you find the information that you are looking for.

THE FIRST PAGE

British computer expert Tim Berners-Lee created the first website in 1991. As people became familiar with web pages and how to build them, they created their own websites. This collection of web pages became known as the World Wide Web. In the early 1990s, there were only a handful of web pages on the World Wide Web. Today, there are billions of pages on almost every subject.

You can access the World Wide Web with the click of a mouse.

THE SEARCH ENGINE BIO

Timothy Berners-Lee was born in London, England, in 1955. In 1980, he devised a computer language called Hypertext Markup Language (HTML) to allow people to share information on the Internet. Hypertext is the interactive text on a computer display. It allows you to click on "hyperlinks" to move around the World Wide Web quickly and easily. In 2004, Queen Elizabeth II honored Berners-Lee with a knighthood for his contribution to computer science.

Tim Berners-Lee designed the computer programs that build web pages.

BEFORE THE WEB

The earliest search engines were invented before Berners-Lee created the World Wide Web. They were used to search public FTP sites—web pages that share computer files over the Internet. They searched for information in a specific place, rather than on the entire web.

People used early search engines to search for computer files on FTP sites. FTP stands for File Transfer Protocol.

ARCHIE

In 1990, computer experts at McGill University in Montreal, Canada, released the first tool to search the Internet. It was called "Archie," which is "Archive" without the "v." Archie created a searchable database of file names on public FTP sites.

NEW SEARCH TOOLS

In 1991, Mark McCahill at the University of Minnesota created a new tool called Gopher to search for files on the Internet. In turn, this led to more sophisticated search programs such as Veronica and Jughead (see below). Despite these developments, by the middle of 1993, no search tool had been created yet for the World Wide Web.

VERONICA AND JUGHEAD

"Veronica" stands for Very Easy Rodent-Oriented Net-wide Index to Computerized Archives. "Jughead" stands for Jonzy's Universal Gopher Hierarchy Excavation And Display. These search programs are named for the characters Veronica and Jughead from the *Archie* comic books.

EARLY SEARCH ENGINES

In September 1993, Oscar Nierstrasz at the University of Geneva in Switzerland developed one of the first basic search engines for the World Wide Web. It was called W3 Catalog.

W3 CATALOG

The search engine W3 Catalog indexed web pages using the information gathered by people searching through the Internet. Its creation led to many competitors, such as Wanderer. This search engine was developed to measure the growth of the World Wide Web. It did so by generating an index called Wandex.

CRAWLING, INDEXING, AND SEARCHING

In December 1993, computer scientists at the University of Stirling in Scotland, the United Kingdom (U.K.), released JumpStation. This combined the three essential elements of a web search engine: crawling (using a computer program to catalog web pages), indexing, and searching. JumpStation searched the Web using the titles and headers of web pages.

A year later, Brian Pinkerton at the University of Washington released WebCrawler. WebCrawler allowed users to search for words within the content of web pages.

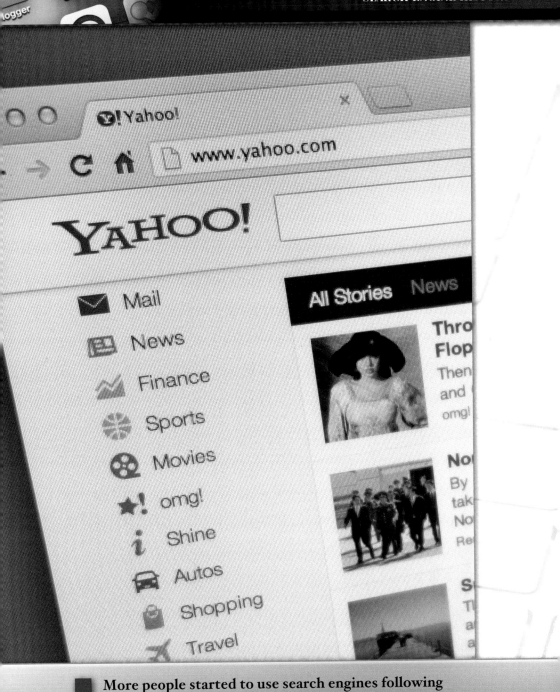

More people started to use search engines following
the release of WebCrawler in 1994. Yahoo! was one
of the most popular early search engines.

MARKET LEADERS

In 1996, Netscape was one of the most popular
Internet browsers people used to search for
pages on the World Wide Web. It gave a higher
ranking to those search engines
that paid Netscape a fee for doing so.

NETSCAPE

The competition between the different search
engines was intense. Eventually, Netscape
decided to promote five different search
engines. They were Yahoo!, Magellan, Lycos,
Infoseek, and Excite. Some of these search
engines are still used today. Others disappeared
in the dot-com bubble. (See next page.)

GOOGLE PAGE RANK

Today, Google is the most successful search
engine. It uses an innovation called PageRank
to index web pages. This feature works by
giving a web page a higher rank if more web
pages link to it. It assumes that better websites
are linked to more web pages. Google lists the
pages in rank order using a browser page.

SUPER SEARCHES

More recently, Microsoft Corporation
launched a search engine called Bing. Yahoo!
now uses Bing search technology.

In 2012, Google created the "Open Drive" search engine, which searches files stored in public data centers, called "the cloud." (Cloud computing is covered in Chapter 5).

THE DOT-COM BUBBLE

In 2000, many search engines disappeared in a financial catastrophe called the dot-com bubble. Before the dot-com bubble, investors put a lot of money into Internet companies. By March 2000, this confidence started to fade. The shares of Internet giant Amazon, for example, plummeted by 80 percent. Amazon survived the dot-com bubble, but many companies did not.

INFORMATION HIGHWAY

In the early days of the World Wide Web, there were only a few web pages with very little content. It was easy to keep up to date—all you had to do was manually browse through a list of all the pages.

COMPUTER INDEXES

By 1993, search engines started to use computer programs instead of people to index the World Wide Web. Early search engines, such as JumpStation and WWW Worm, indexed information using the title of the web pages. As more people published web pages, this method of searching the Internet did not always provide the best results. Soon, new search engines appeared with more sophisticated and efficient searches.

Easy Searches

Today, the World Wide Web is filled with hundreds of billions of pages, which are hosted on tens of thousands of powerful computers called web servers. Search engines provide users with the best results based on the keywords entered. This makes searching for web pages much quicker and easier.

THREE MAIN TASKS

Modern search engines work in different ways, but they all perform three main tasks. First, they use computer programs to trawl through the Internet and identify keywords on web pages. Next, they index these keywords and note where they find them. When you use a search engine, it matches the words you type to the keywords it has indexed. Finally, the search engine provides a list of relevant web pages.

Search engines can help you find the information you need to complete an important homework assignment.

CHAPTER 2

WEB CRAWLING

S earch engines use computer programs called spiders (or software robots—often simply called bots) to search through and index all the pages on the World Wide Web. This process is called web crawling.

A Spider's Journey

Spiders usually start web crawling on popular web servers. They build lists of keywords from web pages, called "seeds," on the servers. The spider then follows every hyperlink on the page. As a result, the spider quickly travels across the World Wide Web, building a huge list of keywords as it goes.

Bot Blocker

In 1993, Dutch-born computer programmer Martijn Koster created a computer program called Aliweb (which stands for Archie-Like Indexing for the Web). Instead of using spiders, Aliweb allowed webmasters to create and submit their own indexes to the search engine. Koster later developed a set of rules for indexing content, which is called the Robots Exclusion Protocol. This allows webmasters to block spiders from their websites.

THE SEARCH ENGINE BIO

Computer expert Matthew Gray created the first web crawler in 1993 while he was studying at the Massachusetts Institute of Technology. He used his bot to power the World Wide Web Wanderer search engine. Gray now works for Google.

An electronic "spider" crawls through the World Wide Web, indexing web pages so you can find them using a search engine.

SEARCH SELECTION

The World Wide Web is so big that even the world's biggest search engines, such as Google, cannot trawl through every single page. It is important that the results of any search contain the best web pages.

SEARCH CRITERIA

Search engines use a complex set of mathematical rules, called algorithms, to index pages on the World Wide Web. The spiders follow these rules and prioritize searches to visit sites that provide the best results. This is known as a selection policy.

The World Wide Web is a vast source of information. Search engines catalog all this data to help you find exactly what you are looking for.

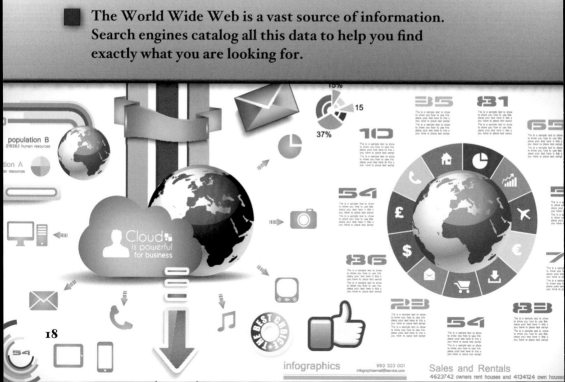

Spider Rules

The first selection policy is to find a good "seed." Algorithms then direct the search to pages that are similar to this starting page. Other rules dictate how the spiders follow hyperlinks to other pages on the Web.

SEARCH SUCCESS

The success of your search depends on the efficiency of spiders crawling the Internet. Here are some of the ways they keep their findings up-to-date:

- Spiders continuously search the World Wide Web for new and updated pages.
- When a spider finds a new page, it indexes the content.
- The spider compares what you type into the search engine with the information on each web page before giving you a list of relevant pages.
- The spider looks at other factors before listing the results. These include how many hits, or visits, the site has received and how many links it contains.
- The search engine may display advertisements alongside the search results. The choice of advertisement often relates to the keywords you enter.

REVISITING SITES

You can find almost anything on the World Wide Web. It is a fast and efficient source of information. Its content is constantly changing.

INFORMATION UPDATE

The information spiders collect can very quickly go out of date. As a result, spiders revisit web pages to index the changes and ensure the information is as current as possible.

FOLLOW THE RULES

Search engines follow two main rules to keep information up-to-date, and to minimize the time between indexing the same page:

- Uniform Policy—A spider visits the same website to index the content at regular intervals. For example, a spider may index websites about rock bands every week. If a band updates its site every day, however, the spider will miss some of these changes.
- Proportional Policy—A spider visits the same website to index the content more regularly if the webmaster often changes the content. For example, if a website is updated daily, a spider will visit it every day to track the changes.

Millions of fans visit websites to follow their favorite musicians, such as Adele. Search engines track any changes on these sites so the information stays up to date.

WHAT'S IN A NAME?

The spiders that power search engines on the Internet have many different names. Googlebot spiders trawl the Internet for the Google search engine, while Yahoo! Slurp is the name of the bot that powers the Yahoo! search engine.

META TAGS

If you develop and publish web pages, you may want to insert Meta tags to help identify your work. These tags often provide web crawlers with the keywords they need to index sites.

MULTIPLE MEANINGS

Meta tags were very useful in the early days of search engines. Think about a website containing words with different meanings.

In the United States, the word "football" refers to a completely different sport than football, or soccer, in England. This is an example of why choosing the right Meta tag matters.

On a website published in England, for example, a "football" fan would be talking about a completely different sport (soccer) than a football fan in the United States. A suitable Meta tag for pages such as these would be "American football."

Meta Tag Decline

Today, webmasters do not use Meta tags as often as they once did. Commercial search engines, such as Google and Yahoo!, rely on other tools to ensure search results remain accurate. Microsoft's Bing search engine still uses Meta tags—but only as a way of detecting junk mail, or "spam."

TAGS TODAY

Search engines use some Meta tags. These tags are unrelated to keywords and include:
- Tags that block crawlers from accessing a page.
- Tags that stop crawlers from indexing a page, but allow them to follow the hyperlinks on the page.
- Tags that allow indexing and access to hyperlinks.

Pay the Price

Spiders can have both a negative and positive impact on a website. However, the disadvantages of allowing web crawlers to index a site may be outweighed by the benefits of making the website more accessible to others.

Slow Down

When a web crawler accesses a website to index the pages, it uses up a lot of web server memory. So anyone looking up information on that web page would find it very slow.

Spider Control

Martijn Koster created the Robots Exclusion Protocol to control how spiders access web pages.

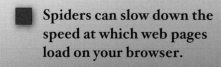

Spiders can slow down the speed at which web pages load on your browser.

If you have a website, you need to consider the advantages and disadvantages of using spiders if you want people to find your site using a search engine.

If you maintain a website, this can be very useful. For example, you may want to restrict access to the site (or certain pages), if you know your site is busy at particular times of day.

PROTOCOL PROBLEMS

Koster's Robots Exclusion Protocol assumes that web crawlers are "polite" and will follow the instructions. However, there is no way of enforcing the rules, and some web crawlers abuse them. Some bots access websites regardless of the rules that protect them.

CHAPTER 3

STORING AND SEARCHING

I magine you are researching your favorite football team. Let's see how you can find out information on the Web using Google.

SEARCH STEPS

These steps assume you have a computer or tablet, such as an iPad, connected to the Internet. Open your Internet browser and type in www.google.com. This will load up the Google search page. Then follow these steps:

- Type in the name of your favorite team, for example, "Miami Dolphins."
- You could add other relevant words such as "football."
- Refine your search by adding keywords, such as "Super Bowl." You do not need to write sentences—just pick out the important words.
- Try using Google's advanced search function if you are having difficulties. Once you have done your initial search, you can access the advanced search by clicking the gear icon near the top-right corner of the page.

BOOLEAN SEARCHES

On most search engines, you can carry out more precise searches using a "Boolean operator." This allows you to refine the way you search for words and phrases.

- If you entered MIAMI DOLPHINS for example, most search engines would carry out three searches—one for MIAMI, one for DOLPHINS, and then again for the whole phrase MIAMI DOLPHINS.
- You can use the Boolean operators AND or + to restrict your search to sites that include both Miami and Dolphins, so you would type Miami AND Dolphins. You can also use OR to widen your search to sites that include Miami or Dolphins, typing Miami OR Dolphins.
- Another pair of Boolean operators are - and NOT, which excludes the term that follows them.

You can type Dan Marino's name into a search engine to find a list of web pages about his amazing career as a quarterback for the Miami Dolphins.

TIPS AND TECHNIQUES

There are various tips and techniques you can use to refine the results of your searches on the World Wide Web. When you become more practiced, you will begin to find information faster than ever before.

QUOTATION MARKS

Quotation marks are a useful tool to narrow down search engine results. On pages 26 and 27, we saw that typing Miami Dolphins into a Google search page would give you any web page containing Miami and it would also give you any page about Dolphins. If you enclose the two words in quotation marks, however, you are much more likely to find pages about the Miami Dolphins football team.

MULTIPLE MEANINGS

Another problem with search engines is words with multiple meanings. For example, if you searched for the word crane, you might get results for a type of bird as well as a lifting machine. You can narrow down the search to pages about lifting machines by adding a minus sign before the item you want to exclude, for example, "crane -bird."

SEARCHING FOR THEMES

Search engines normally give you links to search specific themes, such as current affairs or sports. Here are a few examples of how you might use these functions:

- Most search engines enable you to find news items. For example, to find out what Justin Bieber is doing in the press, you would click on the news search icon and type in "Justin Bieber."
- Another specific search area is a map. If you wanted to see the various countries that make up Africa, for example, you could click on maps and then search for "Africa."
- You can also search for images. This could be useful if you wanted to illustrate a homework assignment.

"Justin Bieber" is one of the most popular search terms on the Web.

STORING RESULTS

Search engines store information found on web pages in useful ways. A search engine might store a list of words and the unique address of the site where they were found.

RANKING

Some search engines give higher value to a word based on where on the page it is found. Others value the number of times a word is found. When you search for a word, the search engine builds a ranking list that presents the most useful pages at the top of the results.

WHAT IS STORED?

Some search engines store all or part of the source page, which is known as a "cache." Others store every word of every page. Once the search engine has searched and cataloged the words, it encodes the information. This is a way of compressing the data. The data is then ready for indexing.

Search engines compress data from web crawlers in much the same way you might compress, or zip, a file before you e-mail it.

When you use a search engine to look for something on the World Wide Web, the search engine trawls through thousands of pages of website data.

LINK ROT

One problem with search engines is "link rot." This happens when a search engine fails to revisit sites regularly, so the content quickly becomes out of date. If this happens, the link in the search results may not work any more. It is then known as a dead, or broken, link.

INDEXING DATA

Search engines use a process called indexing to store the data on web pages in a way that makes it easy for search engines to retrieve.

HASH TABLES

Most search engines use "hashing" to search for information as quickly as possible. This involves distributing words evenly so they are quicker to find. Think of a dictionary. There are far fewer words beginning with "X" than "T," so it is easier to find a word beginning with "X" in a dictionary. Search engines avoid this problem by assigning numbers to each letter. They use hash tables to do this. These tables are an arrangement of words, which are laid out so they are easier to access.

TYPES OF INDEXES

Web crawlers create strings of data as they search through the Web. These strings are known as "forward indexes" but they do not necessarily store data in the best way. Search engines usually rearrange the strings as "inverted indexes," which makes them easier to read and use. Instead of recording words in a particular document, for example, they record documents that use a particular word.

WHAT IS HASHING?

A hash function is an algorithm that maps data and gives it a fixed value. These hash values are sometimes called hash codes or sums. The name of a movie such as *The Lord of the Rings*, for example, can be simplified, or hashed, to make up a simple numerical value. Search engines can quickly search using hash codes.

Search engines store the information from searches, for example, *The Lord of the Rings,* as a sequence of numbers called hash codes.

33

CHAPTER 4

SEARCH ENGINE OPTIMIZATION

A Search Engine Return Page (SERP) displays the results of a web search. This page contains a list of websites in order of relevance to your search. It is sometimes called a web ranking.

HIGH RANKING

Imagine you are a webmaster who has published a new site about the Miami Dolphins. Several sites about the football team will appear in a search engine's web ranking. Most people will click on the link at the top of the SERP—the page with the highest rank. How can you ensure your website has a high ranking?

STEPS TO SUCCESS

Here are a few tips to keep your website up there with the best:

- Use good keywords to attract visitors. The words cannot be too vague or too specific.
- Build links to your site—most pages link only to good sites. Try linking to other pages and inviting sites to link to your pages.
- Ensure you update your website with new and original content, such as the latest player news and game reviews. This is more likely to attract visitors and spiders to index the site.
- Add elements such as discussion threads or forums to encourage fans to leave comments on your website. Doing so will attract visitors.

If you ensure your website is well maintained and current you are more likely to attract a wider audience.

www **Website** Shop

advertisement **Content**
code
Usability optimization
link
building
Design **SEO** keywords

visits hits

TRAFFIC

page rank

■ Search engine optimization increases the
number of visitors to your website by pushing
the site higher up the search engine return page.

Good and Bad

Most webmasters use a technique called search
engine optimization (SEO) to achieve higher
rankings on search engine return pages. SEO
relies on knowing how search engines work.

White Hat

If you are a webmaster with a brand-new
website, you will need to optimize your pages
so your site gets a higher web ranking.

You can adopt good practices, called white-hat SEO, to achieve this goal. Some of these techniques we have already discussed, such as adding keywords, building links to popular sites, and creating interesting content.

Black Hat

You can also try to trick search engines into giving your web pages a higher ranking. This is known as black-hat SEO. One technique is keyword stuffing, which involves filling up web pages with popular keywords that may have nothing to do with the content of your site. Another dishonest method is link farming—when you list links to false websites to improve your ranking. "Gateway pages," for example, are false pages that lead to completely different sites from those noted.

INVISIBLE KEYWORDS

Some webmasters trick search engines by stuffing pages with keywords using invisible text that matches the background color of the page. You cannot see the text, but a web crawler will certainly pick it up.

Many people use the Internet to work at home. All the information you need is at your fingertips using a search engine to navigate the World Wide Web.

OVERCOMING OBSTACLES

Even the most informative and entertaining website may not achieve a high web ranking without using some of the black-hat techniques described on page 37. Of course, everyone wants a successful website, but the way it is promoted is a fine balancing act.

SEO CONSULTANT

Some webmasters use an SEO consultant to promote and improve their site. The consultant looks at different ways to improve the ranking. First, he or she may look at the effectiveness of keywords. The consultant will also look at how the content is organized. The efficiency of rival sites may be compared. A consultant would also check the links and invite other sites to join it.

FUTURE JOBS

The Web is increasingly complex and is growing every day. As a result, it will offer many more job opportunities. In the past, people worked with real things, making products or providing in-person services. Now more and more people are employed in the virtual world of the Internet.

CHAPTER 5

FUTURE SEARCH ENGINES

Twenty years ago, researching a topic for a homework assignment would have meant a trip to the local library to read relevant books. Today, you can often find what you need with the click of a mouse and a search engine.

Concept Searches

Search engines rely on "literal" searches. This means that they look for words exactly as you type them. As a result, they are prone to errors such as spelling mistakes and words with several meanings.

For example, the word "fluke" can be used to mean a fish, a flatworm, the end of an anchor, the fins on the tail of a whale, or a stroke of luck. If you want to find out about the fish, you will not want to see pages that include information about all the other meanings, too.

"Concept searches" aim to overcome this problem by searching for the actual meanings of words rather than simply matching keywords. These searches use complex mathematical techniques to match words in search queries to the results they provide.

Natural Language Searches

Natural language searches are another exciting area of search engine research. They allow people to search websites by asking a question in a similar way to asking a real person. The site www.ask.com works like this, but in a very simple way. Future search engines aim to build more advanced searches that mirror the complexity of everyday speech.

ASK.COM

The search engine www.ask.com (originally known as Ask Jeeves) invites you to ask a question and then tries to provide an answer. If you asked the question, "How far away is the Moon?," for example, it would provide a list of answers as well as a list of relevant websites with more information about the subject.

The website ask.com will tell you that the average distance between Earth and the Moon is 238,857 miles (384,392 km).

Searching the Cloud

People are now storing files on remote machines, referred to as being "in the cloud." Search engines now try to access this new source of information.

Open Drive

As more people store their files in the cloud, the need to search it becomes greater. Google's Open Drive is an example of this. Google wants people to make documents public so

Cloud computing involves storing and accessing files on remote web servers. Modern search engines are now indexing files in the cloud so anyone can search for them.

other people can search for the information they contain. The Open Drive search engine is now available as a Google Chrome App, and for other electronic devices, such as iPhones, too.

PROBLEMS

The cloud is an ideal solution for mobile computing and solves storage problems. However, not all the information stored in the cloud is available to the public. Search engines need to address issues of privacy and access to this information. The real problem is how to control access to data that we do not physically "own." Google has created rules to help people increase the security of the documents they store in the cloud.

PRIVACY ISSUES

In 2011, Chinese computer hackers accessed passwords used by the U.S. government. These sensitive files were stored on remote servers in the cloud. Prior to this, in 2009, a bug in the cloud-based Google Docs app gave people unrestricted access to private data. Examples such as these make many people wary of storing their data in the cloud.

THE WAY AHEAD

As the information revolution continues, we will be able to access more data at faster speeds. Some people think that learning—or at least remembering—will not really matter any more. Why remember vast amounts of information when it is available online?

ARE YOU PREPARED?

Imagine a situation where technological skills are more important than knowledge. It may be a vision of the future, but consider how much has changed in the last few decades. There will be great technological advances in your lifetime. Will you be equipped to deal with this change?

Search engines have changed the way people use the World Wide Web. Who knows where search engine technology may take us in the future?

TOP TIPS FOR USING SEARCH ENGINES

Follow these tips for successful searching:
1. Keep things simple.
2. You do not need to write whole sentences, just pick out the most important words.
3. Use Boolean operators such as AND, OR, and NOT to refine your searches.
4. Use quotation marks to search for whole phrases.
5. For more help with searching, click on the "Help" or "Tips" link on the search page.
6. Used "themed" searches to find different types of content, such as news, maps, or image searches.
7. Try using an advanced search function if you are having difficulties finding what you are looking for.
8. If you are creating a website, include lots of keywords and links to other sites to improve your web ranking on search engines.
9. If you do have a website, ensure you regularly update it with new and original content.
10. Last, but not least: have fun!

algorithms Step-by-step methods for solving problems or accomplishing goals.

black hat Techniques used to trick search engines into giving a site a higher ranking.

Boolean operator A simple instruction for refining a search.

bots Computer software used by search engines to gather and update data—also known as spiders, crawlers, robots, or web bots.

cache All or part of a source page collected by a search engine.

cloud computing Stored data in central systems that users access through the Internet.

File Transfer Protocol (FTP) A way of transferring files over the Internet.

gateway pages Attempts to falsely direct somebody to a web page.

hashing A method of coding information and storing it so that it is easier for search engines to read.

hyperlinks Shortcuts to another web page.

hypertext The text displayed on a browser.

index To gather information by Internet spiders.

Internet A worldwide network of computers.

link farming A black-hat way of attempting to increase the hyperlinks on a website.

link rot A broken or dead link to a website.

meta tags Tags to help search engines index a web page.

Open Drive Google's cloud computing service.

protocol The established set of rules to control the way computers communicate with each other.

Robots Exclusion Protocol The voluntary rules for search engines to follow.

search engine optimization (SEO) The methods used to increase the page ranking of a website.

servers Computers that manage access to services in a computer network.

software The programs and other operating information used by a computer.

spam Junk or unsolicited e-mail.

spiders Software used by search engines to gather and update data—also known as bots, crawlers, robots, or web bots.

trawl To look for something by searching through a large amount of information.

web browser Software that lets users visit web pages and use web applications.

white hat Legitimate techniques used to improve the page ranking of a website.

BOOKS

Graham Gaines, Ann. *Ace Your Internet Research.* Berkeley Heights, NJ: Enslow Publishers, 2009.

Levin, Judith N. *Careers Creating Search Engines.* New York, NY: Rosen Publishing Group, 2007.

Marcovitz, Hal. *Online Information and Research.* San Diego, CA: Referencepoint Press, 2011.

Rabbat, Suzy. *Find Your Way Online* (Information Explorer). North Mankato, MN: Cherry Lake Publishing, 2010.

Sammartino McPherson, Stephanie. *Tim Berners-Lee: Inventor of the World Wide Web* (USA Today Lifeline Biographies). New York, NY: Lerner Publishing Group, 2009.

WEBSITES

Due to the changing nature of Internet links, Rosen Publishing has developed an online list of websites related to the subject of this book. This site is updated regularly. Please use this link to access the list:

http://www.rosenlinks.com/ptech/seng